Key West, I Love You
An Anthology of Love Poems

Key West, I Love You

An Anthology of Love Poems

produced by
The Key West Poetry Guild

Key West, I Love You
Sheri Lohr

Key West, I'm in love with you.
Not like a girlfriend who wants to change you into something new.
Not like a wife who wishes you were like you used to be.
Key West, I love you like a dog does,
just glad to see you every day.
I don't care where you get your money
I don't care who you sleep with
I don't care if you are ethical.
I love you anyway.

I want to sit on the dock
in front of the Schooner Wharf Bar
and look at the color of the finished sunset puddle in the water of the Bight
and I don't care if the color spills around the hulls of shrimpers or yachts.
I am simply delighted at metallic pinks and blues
painting the shapes of miracles.

I want to lie on the beach at Fort Zach
and identify with the flights of gulls
greedy and free and having fun,
claiming raucous credit for their audacious thievery.

I want to pretend I'm a Frigate Bird
whose elegant shape of wing and tail
forms unspoken songs of nautical miles of trackless sea
with a sextant in a nut-sized brain, and ages of ancestral memory.

I want to go to the Green Parrot Bar
and bring home a sailor from some foreign shore.
I will stand up on the stage, and read these lines
and I will bow to the applause of the resolutely un-sober.

Key West, I love you like a dog does,
and I don't really care if you're good or bad,
in fact it all truly means nothing to me,
but I am very glad to see you.
I'll bounce and bark, I'll wag my tail.
I will try to lick your face even if you push me off.

Key West, take me for a walk.

❧ **Frangipani** ❧

❧Orchid ❧

❧ Bleeding Heart Vine ❧

Table of Contents

† **Anthurium** †

Passion/Erotica   64

❧ Bird of Paradise ❧

Joyful   83

Acknowledgements

With gratitude and affection we of the Key West Poetry Guild acknowledge the following poets and friends of poets for their invaluable time and energies devoted to creating this, unique to Key West, anthology of love poems.

First, to Richard and Suanne Hatch for their generosity in donating the space for the Guild to meet every month upstairs at their restaurant, Blue Heaven, on Petronia Street, Key West, as well as for their sponsorship of this anthology and for the delectable refreshments they serve us at every Guild meeting.

Thanks are also due to these supporters and contributors:

To Allen Meece, poet and longtime Guild member, for working so hard to get this project started.

To the KWPG Anthology Editorial Board: C.S. Gilbert, Allen Meece, Leonel Valle, Nance Boylan, Susan Steves and Alex Symington.

To Anna Symington for her pre-publishing organizational skills of which there are many.

To Fran Decker for the beautiful cover art, depicting our home at Blue Heaven.

To Sheri Lohr, poet, longtime Guild member and publisher, for so lovingly putting all the pieces together.

To Kirby Congdon for the concise and intelligent forward to this book.

And special thanks to the thirty-eight poets who have contributed their work and poetically testified for love in all its forms.

To our readers, we hope that YOU will find love in Key West. We have.

Introduction

Since the very word, "anthology," comes from the Greek term for a flower garland, the editors here have, appropriately enough, looked at this garland with keen eyes. While poems are seldom written to order to fit a category, the reader may still like to know what kind of poem he may expect. Here, in this anthology, we have a grouping of ideas and feelings that lend themselves to a stance that relates poems to each other without a loss of individuality or originality. This helps us pick up on the particular poet's language more quickly and lets us plunge into the nectar of the flower for its essence, to turn a flowery phrase. So, a rare perfume may be only a matter of smell rather than one of taste, and we won't mention color, but that is for the reader to decide.

Kirby Congdon

Chapter 1

Frangipani

Close to perfect

Valentine's Day, years on…
Rosalind Brackenbury

There doesn't seem to be a card
which says, I have loved you
more than anyone; something
about the tense perhaps
puts greeting card makers off.

There isn't a card either
which says, I still love
you but differently. Or to say,
I will love you
probably forever
but not necessarily
in your company.

I can't find a card to say,
maybe if we separated then
became friends?
Or, how about a divorce?
Or, will you have dinner
with me sometimes,
and sometimes watch movies
and dance?

And can we cry and laugh
in the small hours,
holding hands?

Or to say, whenever I see a cat
prowling the street I will say hello
to it and think of you,
and when I hear a mockingbird
or an osprey's whistle
and whenever I smell jasmine

on the street –

I'm glad there isn't a card
to say any of what I really mean
or what you mean to me
and never will be.

Goodbye Passion (Flower)
Cricket Desmarais

Within the week, the spiked bright bodies
creep across the vines of our passion
flower, a gift we thought fit for winter

solstice, the day when light leaks
in at low doses and leans towards the promise
of more. Weeks later, the purple blooms

stop blooming. Gone are the exquisite wispy—
nippled petals turning themselves towards the sun,
leaves left ratty and tattered by hungry caterpillars.

Like most things, it is difficult to appreciate
what will come later. Bright yellow eggs
scatter on the trellis and stems. We won't see

them blacken or hatch, nor is there any remnant of
eggshell. It devours that, too. We miss the shudder
and jiggle of skin being shed, the exoskeletal

spilt, like a sleeve removed and left on the fine
slick of silk that keeps it from falling. Larva
to pupa, caterpillar to chrysalis—all the while

the Gulf Fritillary feeds with ferocity. We wait
for our own forms to change. Call it pathetic
metaphor, but the cliché lives within this limp

plant propagating something other than itself.
And because we bought it, brought it home, potted
and watered it, trained it to trail up the wooden slats—

I believe it must be telling us something, maybe
even to be more like it—willing to shed everything.
I am a poet, after all, and live by the small world's

tall orders. By spring, we learn to love the shambles
of what it is—a ragged plant with suspicious critters
brazenly grazing upon it. The sun shines in through the tears

and tatters and turns the diapause of camouflaged
curl golden. In nature's perfect moment of knowing,
the chrysalis cracks open, flies free.

Key West
Leonel F. Valle

There's an absence
in me.
Because of you?

From the south window
I gaze on a green wall
of tall ancient mangoes,

swaying softly to
the fresh new breeze
of an unexpected
but welcomed season.
At night,
a concert of doves
arrives at my bed,
lulling me to sleep.

Or is someone
whispering my name?

Still,
this blue absence
haunts me.

Where are you?
And where
is the sea?

Redox Pair
Susan S. Keiser

Easy enough to put it all down to a rust of nails,
or maybe to a bed of nails, if we take a
less-oxidized point of view.

Corrosion had always seemed a small price to pay,
and distant: electron transfer seemed so remote in the
newness of mirror-bright mornings and maybe
the rains would never come, and maybe we would
always see ourselves this way, unreduced
but forever on the brink of
bursting into flames.

Remainders
Malcolm Willison

Late afternoon of instant left–
overs, yet by sundown
she who cooked them
will be even farther
than her departure down the street
in a pink taxi to the usual
airline to the rest of Florida and a cold north.

Already since I've waved her off
I've met faces new to me
around our street, helpful in concern
for trash removal. (For which
they've kept an eye out
but never seen me.)

And she will call in haste again
(against the clamor of Miami
and my nap from her)
yet ask me to lower my voice
over the brief wires.

Her half the bathroom sink
and closet already four hours empty
an unlikely wind
has shifted to the west
so that another arriving bank
of clouds will blush in sunset
while I remember her
into the cooling night.

A Friend Speaks of Unrequited Love
Tod Perry

Unrequited love is to life
the tender inside of an oyster,
a private room not living in
fully until once emptied.
It grows as a pearl upon the heart,
to the weight of a manhole cover
that time cradles no matter how heavy,
yet opens one day in the early mists
as a carapace to be shed
into a merge of sorrows and suggestions,
shadows that surprise us and walk
with us ever before and behind
from one room to the next.

When Love Dies
J.M. Varela

Falling in love in Key West
Is just as thrilling
As it is in so many other romantic places.
Your heart still skips a beat
When he comes into the room.
Holding hands in an outdoor café
Gazing in each other's faces.

The difference is
When love dies in the tropics
You don't stay depressed
For too long.
How could one stay sad
With the sun shining so brightly
Sprinkling diamonds of light
Here and there in the blue green ocean.
Creating a distraction, at the very least,
For a broken heart.

Orange pink sunsets hang on the horizon
Soft and warm like comforting arms.
When sleep does not come,
Silvery moonlight reflects off metal roofs
Gently moving your heart
To a more peaceful place.
A subtle reminder that tomorrow will bring
Another awesome sunrise
Another reason to love again.

Give Me No Tomorrows
Allen Meece

Give me no chronometers
marking time.

Give me no tomorrows,
today is mine.

And if she leaves on Wednesday
or a month away from June,
give me no tomorrows
for I have had the moon.

And give me no great distance
my weary feet to tread
for I shall keep those yesterdays
that we have spent in bed.

doing time
Katherine Doughty

someone dropped the clock.
the copper-tops rolled across the floor.
the clatter woke the sleeping couple.
oh well, their time was up anyhow.
someone dropped the clock,
the face fell off time and
caused a wrinkle, there, between her brows.
up until now it had always been
four minutes earlier inside the shell
than on the sand or in the surf.
only from inside could they experience
its hard spiraling curl as an endless wave
inside, the train was forever arriving at the station.
the passengers lingered over tea (sugar in the spoon)
and a pastry (yes fresh this morning) before boarding.
life inside the shell was calmly measured
until she wanted to taste the sea,
and he needed to melt the sand,
then, it was too late.

Late night poem
Nance Boylan

I'll breathe you in
but I'll let you out.

I'll hold you close
but I'll let you go.

I'll take your hand
but I'll walk alone.

I'll fill your dreams
but I'll wake you up.

I'll stir your desire
but I'll calm you down.

I'll cradle your body
but I'll go home.

I will, I think
or maybe, I'll just go to sleep.

Tin-roof cradle
Susan S. Keiser

1.
Surveyed by orange moons
and all-night garbage lullabies,
a mangrove cuckoo croons
her dock-blue reggae,
small mockery
of a streetwise cockerel,
crowing his free-range love
in midnight lanes

2.
Sweet pandemonium is the
wrong side of sundown;
 no country for quiet men,
this, a silence drowned
by alley wars,
the feline mimicry of
babes that cry 'murder'
by moonlight,
 gypsy birds in foul streets,
strutting shameless
with moon-hatch chicks
and seething at
the cool, indifferent stars

3.
Moon-shook rock-a-byes
exact their vivid toll on
summer sleepers;
they are restless,
tossing under clammy sheets.
Far above, the loose-limbed giants
release their fragile hold, heaving

wind-whipped crash and roll
to shatter night; to
rock these tin-roof cradles
in the dark

Key West, in Another Neighborhood
Vicki Boguszewski

The day is very young,

It holds enormous potential;

While we remain self-contained:

A troop of artists, contraband smugglers, retirees, self-help junkies, and the new age enlightened.

Morning smells of Cuban coffee and Nag Champa, a never-ending stream of dog walkers, a handful of Bubbas drinking shots of bucci on the corner from a shared cup, the newspaper box their service counter.

Frangipani and Jasmine stings my senses with sweetness, wraps me in a Key West moment I can now securely never leave behind.

Duval Street Gal
Leonel F. Valle

A northwest wind
whips around
building corners,
scattering the red leaves
of the almond trees.

I think of you
waiting tables
in the noisy café
on Duval Street,

blue jeans and sandals,
an easy smile
for the pleasure of
friends and strangers,

while I wait for you,
lonely and jealous,
at the old loft
in the Bahama Village,
writing bad poetry.

My Second Spring
Eric Brockmyer

Winter blown cold, across gray white-capped water
Strangling waves absolute stalk life's daughter.
Cold, lonely, bereft, barren shores cry out fallen
No promise nor future, eyes silent and frozen

Sudden warm breeze, warming first robin's call
Calm zephyr wind, gracing my path's heart fall.
A second's brief glance, celestial equinox wonder
Energy, passion, and fire to ponder

My second spring came late in life's passing season
Irrational thoughts, energy, reason
A fire spring thaw and beautiful breeze
Carefully opening flowers released

A sweet robin heralds life's second spring
Lightening step, bright ecstasy ring
Happily forward, loving divine
Hoping that Spring fills the rest of our time.

For a Friend
Kirby Congdon

This is where you lay your head

and left your body's scent

on the spent folds of the random sheets

abandoned, in their disorder,

on a vacant bed.

Here, in these rooms,

the air, weightless, carries voices

across the endless length

of a season's afternoon.

Through those windows the light

flowed and, slanting,

described a moment's pose

before your face, turning,

fell into the secrets of its own shadow.

My hand can still feel

your fingers' grip

when daylight never came

and the sun was a lightning's flash

in a stormless night.

Even our dreams, disarrayed became bizarre.

Order took vacations beyond their normal days;

so here we are, conjoined, as if together,

for an age, the two of us

spellbound yet singularly estranged.

Chapter 2

Orchid

Beauty & Strength

Astral Light
(Cardinal, Fixed, Mutable)
Sheri Lohr

For my lovers in the dawn
I was the shattered glass edge of Venus rising in the east,
    a bright revelation in the blue end of night
    caressing the disappearing secrets of darkness.
I was the brightest thing in the sky, before the birth of day
    bled into heaven's natal pool,
    dilute rose transubstantiating into golden wine.
I was amazed at my own newness,
innocent in nascent light,
for my lovers in the dawn.

For my lovers under the sun
I was light refracted through the leaves of trees.
    I was sunburn on my own breasts
    warm on someone's cheek in a shady place.
I shed enough light to open every flower
    in unfenced fields, or cracks in the walk,
    or pots on a curtained sill.
The color of every bloom was my laughter.
My heat beaded the skin
of my lovers under the sun.

To my lover as the light is melting
I am colors without names before the sunset burns,
    as elusive as effervescent light broken on the face of the sea,
    the tarnished gold of broken idols, prepared for refining fire.
I am the mutable light that flatters any portrait
    from a source outside the frame;
    changing light on a window seen from a lawn below.

Suspended like a bubble in the fluid amber afternoon,
I reach with my stretching shadow
to the lover who will find me in starlight.

Hummingbird
Alex Symington

Lifting my heart

over a wall

to feel the rough

stone of it

against me

At the top

I see that you

have turned

to mist

Your eyes are smoke

Your skin

hot vapor

Your storm cloud

rains on my wall

My heart

is condensed,

beating like a

Hummingbird.

Solstice
Rosalind Brackenbury

It arches our yard, both close and far,
a watery rainbow sewing up the sky;
you call me from bed to see
I in my nightdress barefoot on grass,
half sleeping still, the rainbow
surprising me awake. In bed
again with tea and book I feel
the scratch of grass still
in my soles, wet earth rushing up
through me, you with an arm
around me in the soaked dawn.

Pink
Cricket Desmarais

Pink, I think. My mind races with its color,
of things we tend to think sweet: fragrant mimosa
fluttering with bees, the cat's sandpaper tongue
licking herself clean, the five starry-armed starfish
in the shallows of sea. But don't think of pink as a
always soft or sweet. No, these pinks are not just
lacy ruffle on a schoolgirl's sweater, the cute hat Aunt
Maude made you for your baby-girl-to-be. Pinks can be brave
and benevolent, too, like the inside of conch mollusk,
slipping across benthic bottoms or blown during warfare
or worship, it's top sawed off, calling all the Gods
to their side. A ribbon attached to where a breast
once was, the video we watched, the newborn crossing over
into our oxygen through the ripe, pink cervix, thrashing
in her own pink newness until tucked up and suckling,
the deep pink of placenta expelling itself. Today it's the rash
that creeps across my face, a sweeping, itchy pink of hormones,
hustling up the day of my own swelling belly's labor
and delivery. My midwife tells me this girl is flamingo-
footed inside of me, her knee juts out, presses into
my right side, digging into ribs that evolution tells me
did not come from Adam. Look around: we were all born
from pink, some mother that made us, let us free from
pink canals and purple folds or a long slice down an abdomen,
plucked up and out from an amniotic liquid of love.
I cannot say how this child will arrive, though I hope she will fly
out like those pink birds, gregarious waders that can swim
or float when the water gets too deep, drink salt, excrete
through glands, travel great lengths to get where they need
to go. Now she hiccups, her lungs strengthening for the day
she will breathe on her own, clasp her pink mouth on my pink

breasts and drink until we are both washed in pink dream. Think pink, says the dream, before she came to be. Before we all came to be. Before we all came to be, the pink stiff of his and the first pink wink and shiver of what only a woman can know, can grow.

Equinox: Brief Encounter
Malcolm Willison

I am waiting
at the Aqueduct Authority
for the cab I'll take
to meet you, who's been watching
over your mother-in-law,
at the aiport where the plane
will curve down
over the old coral town's
abandoned salt flats, cisterns
and the birds.

I've missed you
under palms and frangipani
as I've strolled up the streets
with our friend, who turns his head
at pretty boys and muscles.
I keep an eye for restaurants;
galleries, too, attract my glance, gliding
off mannequined bikinis
and hard smooth plastic torsos
in stylish windows.

Now a flight's arrived.
but it is late, a woman says
and I am early. Still, I too look,
among the crowd seeking luggage
and transport. Will I mistake
some spectacled, compact blonde
in pants for you? Or temporarily believe
I recognize a beauty smiling
back into some husky face?
and what of the wide-spaced eyes

resembling your collegial enemy—
though not a woman's—picking out his baggage?

Tonight we'll together saunter after supper
through warm streets like wary cats
under dark wisteria. I will be back
here at the airport in two days' time
going through security to leave you
behind again, to replace you
at my mother's side at home.

Olivia Street Prayers
Susan S. Keiser

Tiny cups of bucci, and I walk the backstreets.
Christmas palms sway with languid goodwill,
inclining slightly in a tin-roof rain; raucous,
an autumnal assault on our wetter lanes.

The autumn winds we name, more often than not.
Nail up all the doors. Then nail up all the windows.
Kneel with tiny flames to Mary, Star of the Sea.
In autumn we trust in kneeling, and in nails, for love.

Unraveling
Nance Boylan

I bend like ribbon
under your translucent weight,
move with unspoken rhythm
there is no space between us-
all secrets are hidden.

I have no sense to recognize your spell,
your immoral gaze
perfectly timed kisses whisper lies
beneath my skin
I listen intently for the words
meant just for me.

High among the marbled clouds,
rich with our songs, I dream of
unraveling in the noon sky, amidst
the static of lost time
where memories fade…

Unquenching
Flower Conroy

Mind dipped in fairy tale slumber–crystal formation
within the disc of an erupting star–you dreamt
     upon ocean, rocked into nap by liquid arms–
Andromeda ship's unexplored cradle.

I sponged afternoon, absorbed the view: across water's
surface sunshine dazzled–mercury beading with each
     wave's blistering, hypnosis of drowning
unremembered kaleidoscopic warped pattern.

Yesterday I overhead a stranger call the blue of this met-
amorphous pool miraculous & I contemplated:
     stars' dark star wombs; blue-green atmosphere;
cosmic seeds dividing; sprouts sprouting; that

succulent sound. I imagined vineyards lifting smog veils
with damp fingers; I concocted waterfalls of lava
     thickly smudging jungle mountainsides
of a curled, rooted island–then coagulating

into beds of cobalt ash. Dusty dead stars. The color
of the post-equinox. The hemispheric longitude
     of Venus. Lunar mountains.
You sighed. I ached to steal a sip of your lips...but my

drizzle touch awoke you. Beheld by archipelago, sunspot
flecked satellite eyes–they mirrored volcanic firebody
     so that I swallowed deep, thirst-struck, whet for you,
while the world surrounding lapped patiently
against the parched, evaporating infrared aghast light.

Hope Deferred
Lucy Miranda

What almost is, but isn't, hurts
It stabs, stings and squeezes
Pressing patience out
An unsought yearning teases
I dare not tell you
Can't you see?
My eye's on you...
Is yours on me?
And if it is, and if you care,
Why are you still just standing there?
I Wait for your Love,

I remain rock steady,
My eye fixed till he's ready;
I'm waiting still

Eyes on Him, I'll wait until
What almost is, but isn't, Is.

How I Loved You
Steve Allerton

I will build a house
And keep a warm white room
Where you can sleep
Where troubles melt away
Like flakes of snow

Where every morn
My kisses take
The crust that your enchanted dreams
Make in your eyes
So when you wake you'll know

That I love you
That I love you
That I love you

Years will fly
And we will lie
Upon that bed
And I will buy you
Sweets and fruits
And all that you desire
Exploring every crevice of your frame
Gently whispering you name
I promise I will never tire

Of loving you
Of love
Gently loving you

For I have known the taste of time
Upon your lips
Your tender kiss
Don't want to miss

A day away from you

I want to go upon this voyage bold
Feeling young and growing old
To share each day with you anew

And when my weary bones expire
Cast them off upon the funeral pyre
A burning fire for all to see

My love for you will still be burning bright
My adoration in the night
A gift for you to remember me.

And how I loved you
I loved you
How I loved you

Icarus

Sarah Goodwin-Nguyen

We've reached the cooling point
Which comes after the first hot,
Luscious plums of summer
Days are slow and patient,
Not I, nor the grace with which
You've entered in – O big eye
Why are we waiting?

First our wings are skin and air
You steal kisses in my neck and hair
Later our backs are flesh and leather
My hands are ruined with the work
Lips become wax and clay, eyes
Painted on, the lighting frames
An episode of surrender
Disgraceful, this fall to earth

WD40 For My Soul
Ray Campbell

The telescope of my dreams
is focused on your light.
On fragile wings of trust,
The long lost ghost of my savior
Is reflected in your eyes.
Hope, a long missing companion,
Revisits my heart and
Doors that were rusted shut yesterday,
Open without a sound.

Reality & Dreams
J.M. Varela

When these karmic chains
That bind me to this ground
Have all been worked away
By lessons of laughter and tears.
Then, only then, will my restless spirit
Be set free–heaven bound.

Up through the clouds and sky of blue
Past the ionosphere, moon and stars.
There in the fathomless void of space,
Somewhere between the galaxies,
I will wait for you.

The, together again,
Joining hearts and hands
We will fly throughout the universe,
We'll visit every star system
And watch as new worlds are born.
We'll leave no light unseen.
Our love will shine across eternity
As no sun has ever shone.
Guiding others through the fantasy of death
To the reality of their dreams.

Valentine's Day at Sea
Sara Shea

Placid Atlantic at dusk
reminds of love –
a ship's mast thrust
through the setting sun.
Sails slice the sky;
white wings of a dove.

On the Brink of White Coral
Theresa Carr

Like that color,
when you take a left at Sawyer Key,
Cudjoe channel.
You are drawn to stop
Or get there at all costs.
To look at it.
Take it in
And let it expand.
To always keep it
And hold on to it before...

Like that water,
South of Shark River,
When it's so still, so calm
Coming across the Gulf.
The passing of the boat
Undulates softly in glazed ripples,
Smooth, silky,
A woman's hips and form,
Over and over and over.
The touch of your lover.

Or when the day's end sunlight
Glistens in molten glass crystals,
A layer on top of the sea,
First blues then greens then goldens.
I want you here,
And I'm holding on
Till we swing around on the anchor.

Methods
Alex Symington

You are the poet

I love.

Far away stare

from far away.

So tender a creature,

teaching varied

methods of cat skinning

and anthropological

bloodletting.

You startle words

to stampede pages,

a riot of beautiful

violence.

I am your rapt student.

I will share my

rusty time machine,

if only to see

your future.

Thomas Street
(For Ray 3/27/00)
C.S. Gilbert

On his 72nd birthday, bewitched, she noticed
he was embodiment
of those tawny bronze bantam roosters,
ubiquitous on Thomas Street—
and he was wiser (some would say
more beautiful) than she.
So she listened carefully.
"After mid-life," he said,
"we learn to love that which is kind.
Passion sleeps then, and the blood cools."
She believed him.
He was wrong.

Before "The Day"
Carol Fran

In private we marry—
one to the other

No one else attends—
or is needed.

Consummation
      is not our cry.

Commitment
      is our song:
      to help,
          honor,
              protect,
                  love...
and all else
we'll ever need.

There will be ceremonies
      for the dreams of others.
But they are of little matter.
We've already married -
one to the other.

Only a Woman
Ray Campbell

Like a good conversation
She excites you and makes you think,
Makes you dream,
Makes you better.

In a town of women
With hearts that beat like mountains,
She is a she-wolf howling at the moon.

She is like Virgilio's cheesecake,
Sweet to the tongue,
And everyone in the room is jealous
When they see she is there for you.

In a town of women
With dreams so strong they breathe on their own,
She is a dream and a prayer already answered.

Like a cafe con leche
She is hot and strong, creamy and sweet
She warms you all over
With the very first taste.

In a town of women
With souls that rage like flowers,
She is a summer shower and the rainbow.

Her eyes dance all around her laughter
Her smile is moonlight on the water
I could live forever in those eyes.
In that smile.

You can say she is only a woman.
I say,
She is a goddess.
She makes me dream.
She makes me hope,
She makes me...
Better.

At the Edge
Kirby Congdon

I know the face,

the contours of the brow,

chin, cheek, and jowl,

but now I only see

your neck's nape

where we sit, hip to knee

on the steep steps

leading down, against the west,

to the endless stretch

of the beach's empty feast

of sky, tide, and the single grains,

abandoned, and uncounted, of sand.

Your body, familiar,

at the edges of my finger tips

quiet my mute alarms

in the comfort seen

in the great greed

of my cataleptic arms.

Sharon
Mark Burgin

Her Beauty is like the vastness of the ocean, wild crazy blue madness

Her scent is of fresh ginger and salt water, refreshing and calming my restless soul

She is soothing and clean like a crisp, cool fall morning with bright yellows and swirling browns

And my mind races for answers, while my heart thumps wildly

But, I can taste her breath in the wind; feel her warm embrace in the ocean

And I know serenity is mine.

Through the White Linen
Eric Brockmyer

Through the white linen, your soul stands clear
As fine and as sharp as in your younger year;
With closed sleeping eyes and finely combed hair
Not dulled by the solemn pall in the air

I remember your grace, and the tender ease
For soft, quick embraces and kisses like breeze
And gone away are the less noble and rotten
Forever banished, and all but forgotten

And together we danced, and sang and played
And loved till the morning light long strayed
And loved still deeper as time marched in
Until under white linen, we meet again.

Island of You
Steve Allerton

I always wanted to sail on the ocean
To follow my wandering star
To go with the wind where it takes me
No matter how distant or far
So I went out one day to the forest
To cut a tall sturdy mast
Wild oak trees feel to make me a schooner
And I built it so graceful and fast

And I went with the tide and the current
And I followed my compass so true
And I went where my wandering star told me
Till I came to the island of you

So I went out one day from the harbor
With the wind at my back from the start
The dolphins and birds gave direction
On my voyage to follow my heart

And after many long days of wandering
Being hit by a tempest or two
Your seagulls appeared in the rigging
And your mountains came into view.

Saying Au Revoir
(for Pam)
C.S. Gilbert

Sometimes the chalice is too full to touch,
thin skin of pressure holding more a measure
than we know, a fullness too complete for words.
Some friendships are like that.

In that perfect balance, perfect calm,
sleeps the potential of the storm: one or
the other will burst out, driven like horses,
or the winds and rain of hurricanes,

elemental forces in the face of something
small and peaceful, curling up within. I know
that place in you, and you in me. Let's wish
no more gale winds to strip the varnish off

that weathered wood, so now will come
sweet zephyrs of the spring before the summer,
just when lambs (newborn) and we (set free)
come out to play. Until that spring

I hold you in my heart.

At Key West Bight
Rosalind Brackenbury

Here is our life,
the water blue in winter,
the boats and pelicans,
the island where we married;
there, the gas dock
we left from all those years ago,
I in my white dress,
you in your silk shirt,
flowers in your buttonhole;

the course we took between shallows,
to cross the ship channel
the schooner I worked on,
the harbor where we scooted
among yachts,
in our old boat, with its
captious engine, its V-berth
for love and quarrels;

today in noon-day sun
we sit aloft in the sunset bar,
the only ones here;
fish and chips
and tea our feast; we eat
with our fingers, don't
talk seriously.

I have forgotten
anything I wanted other than
your presence, you have forgotten
the perfect woman I never was.
Finally there's no agenda: just
a view.

Chapter 3

Bleeding Heart Vine

Love Lost

On a Death
Kirby Congdon

As even weeds come to flower
and those blossoms go to seed,
so, too, the dust of their roots
is scattered in a silence
across the cavern of your room.
My fist grips the blight
that has left each sense bereft
in this darkness at noon.
I have knowledge now
that neither of us knew before
of how we're picked of all our fruit
and rudely plucked of the very bloom
our two lives, gifted, grew.
My empty arms hug the air
yet I feel your body's bones
evident everywhere.
An unreachable distance can
appear, somehow, near
as an absence, too,
can be now, and here.

Winter
Leonel F. Valle

Too bad you came
so late into my life,

when silver green tarpon
vanish to seek the warm
twilight of the deep channels,
and a cold wind that
blows from the north
burns the cocoplums

and browns the leaves
of the sea grapes,

and when a long winter
of the years gone by
has frozen my heart.

In the Pink Morning Hour
Nance Boylan

Love, I used to be in one piece, whole
before you found me.
Solitude suited me (I told myself).

Now, tangled in thought,
I can feel my heart rupture
in the pink morning hour.
In pain, it sits in tatters.
I ache in places I didn't even know I had.
This constant state of perpetual anguish
confuses my inner compass.
I am in that in-between place, where seasons collide,
perturbed, humorless.

Love, you bring along your companions with you,
fear, anxiety, uncertainty.
You justify hatred, warrant my bitterness.

Oh love, you disappoint me, again...
I will miss you.

Phoenix
J.M. Varela

A coward she must have been
To be so frightened.
Or, perhaps just a very gentle soul
Who stood in awe while in his presence.
Having opened Pandora's Box,
She trembled when its contents were revealed.
How can one being possess so much feeling?
The intensity of it takes the breath away
And stops the heart from beating.
The moth was only scorched by the flame.
And now wonders
Will she ever have the
Courage and strength to get lost
In the fire of his soul?
Then, on the other hand,
Like the legendary Phoenix
She will arise,
Reborn in youthful freshness
From her own ashes.

Catch and Release
Katherine Doughty

I am tired of catch and release
I did my part
I swallowed your hook
it is your turn now
sharpen your knife
and take my scales

I have been thrown back
so many times
I am too old for this school
the others eye my scared smile
with a certain awe
but mostly pity
we swim flashy ancient dances
which I have also grown tired of

I am between two worlds
having fallen from the nest
into the sky
my mother doesn't want me anymore
dry land seems no kind of life either
but maybe
a good place to die
smothered in buere blanc
melting in your mouth
finally caught
and released

If Only You Knew
Omar Calleja

If only you knew what I've gone through
The things I thought I knew and withdrew
Wasted years and evaporated tears never ceasing
Yet pain mingled with Joy ever increasing
Oh if you only knew...

I wonder where you are tonight
only the moon can see you
They're playing some of our songs somewhere
and I here alone so blue
You haven't changed at all in my mind still smiling there
That's the way I will always remember you so near
Oh if you only knew...

I know that I have been changed by Heaven's Hound
He has fixed my heart by His Word now bound
Today I am loving Him much more
And my love for you is but an inordinate affection
That love that continues to linger there an eternal reflection
Oh if you only knew...

The years grow longer but the distance remains the same
(the past is never that far behind)
You're there, me here somewhere twain
To see you once again is my secret desire (God knows)
To relive for just a moment that youthful fire.
Oh, if you only knew...

Long Love
Pam Strother

To have courage when my lovers are dying is a dangerous
         thing.
Old men now turned to ashes are sprinkled on a tepid sea
where once we rocked each other in passion and in sleep.

I keep alive their sets of lips, so sweet and soft,
in dreams musty with decades of longing,
the longing of myself, the longest lived.

In the dark quilt-wrapped cocoon of midnight mind
         wandering,
I feel again the gulf breeze that reeks of wind-whipped
         rides in first cars
and slow dancing and hot jazz in trendy clubs.

The fire that fueled us squats smoldering on a beach long
         washed away,
brave remnant of the strength of memory.
I still try to rely on the long future even here at the end of
         the road.

Only the little lapping wavelets incessant on the sand
convince me
that I won't be left behind.

Orchids at Midnight
Deborah C. Linker

After the rain,
orchids at midnight
reach out to me
in the warm wet darkness.

Crickets chirp, fish jump
as the soothing night air
washes over me.

Memories lying here
under the dancing stars,
ignites a wild passion

your warm kisses
on the small of my neck,
two young and careless lovers
lost in touch

a white orchid
on my bare skin
as you kissed away
the sprinkles of rain.

Locked in the pain of losing you
I am forever
tethered
to these delicate orchids at midnight.

bougainvillea
Katherine Doughty

you sent bougainvillea from mexico
dried up
seeming fragile
still brilliant
spilling from the envelope in vermont
singing a far away song
i live here now
an island laden with trees
the city is movement and noise
dirty alive with its thorns
they catch you in the cheek
as you make your way
along her broken paths
this tree this life
in fuchsia white
pink purple and orange
keeps going through war and pain
though we've given up so many times
trying to connect
we know our souls too well
know we will once again dig through
trash to recover the shiny part
declare desires through broken windows
and stop buses which are speeding
away with lovers
we cannot not bear to lose

On opening mail from Joanie on Friday
Pam Strother

Your letter said you are about to die.
Your strength and speech are gone, and breath is short.
The doctors don't know how or what or why.
No diagnosis sums up their report.
Because they cannot find out what is wrong,
your life is ending long before it should.
My friend, I mourn the loss of your heart's song
and rue the loss of all your work for good.
There for your weddings and for Jason's birth,
there, too, for many ups and downs since then,
what I'll remember is our joy and mirth
and how our closeness always bloomed again.
My grief groans loud with sorry letting go.
Such early death. Oh, Joan, I'll miss you so .

If I Could Trade
Lisa Ermine

As a small child, knowing not then
The years to come, the emptiness within,
For all the riches I possess
Can and do not fill that emptiness.

If I could trade, just for a moment
To see her face, not in a photograph,
If I could only feel her hand
Instead of the frame's glass.

Although my God has taken
I still cannot let go,
I need more than my best, for it's not enough
To forget that woman, I don't even know.

Could the love be so great
Since 30 years have passed,
Will 60 years still be the same
Will my flag still then, fly half mast?

Strong as Lily
Deborah C. Linker

Be strong they said, when I was only three,
wiping my cheeks as mama drove away.
You're strong, she needs me
said my young blond lover
when he left me at thirty-three.

Broken trust,
tears and lies
as pieces of my heart disappear
along life's cutting trail.

Be strong as Lily Bow
in the billowing winds of Cudjoe
growing limes to survive
and living off the sea.

Strong-willed she was
when her booze-loving man
hit the Northern road,
leaving two sons and a wife
among the mucky mangrove.

Years later
with thickened heart
and lost key,
I reach out with love,
But make sure nothing touches me.

Like Lily Bow,
at nature's heart
in the smudge fires of Cudjoe,
I am strong, I am brave and
I am
alone.

For Ralph Simmons, Jr.
(11 October 1932 - 6 November 2009)
Kirby Congdon

Each nail that you hammered down

to hold the parts of this house in place

supports this bending body's bones

as your deft hand enhanced the fine details

where the slow timbers rose like cornerstones

from an ocean's spread of sand.

And so the quiet focus in your steady eye

let me also rise to be who I am

and, finally, learn to perform

the hard chores taken on

in the hollow storms of this silent tide

of confusion's time where I practice how

one stands alone to prove

the deep foundations' depths

of your very name engraved

on my own life's flesh

as I try living out a meaning for both our lives

that may flow, fresh or even wise,

from beyond the drift of the backwash, spent,

spilling out from that timeless time

of your untimely death.

Chapter 4

Anthurium

Passion/Erotica

Blue Sandals
Leonel F. Valle

Sandals laced
of thin leather strips,
her pale feet
appear more naked
than they are.

A turquoise asp
loops her toe,
 moves up the arch
of the bare foot,
and encircles her ankle,
a willing slave.

Foreign and exotic,
blue sandals that
evoke lost palaces
in mighty Babylon
or the Hindustan,
where veiled dancers
whirl to the beat
of tribal drums
for the pleasure of
cruel masters.

Her face, her walk
I no longer recall,
her blue sandals
haunt my dreams.

Precious Luscious
Flower Conroy

My mango sack sizzles with fruit
flies, a wasp or two,
a few curious bees.
Under sun's steady monocle eye
my skin glows
rose nettle.

Already my tongue stings
with too much mango.
Squash-
colored threads
embedded between teeth.

Overindulgence buzzing
in my brain: razzled
ant colony dismantling
a sugar cube, sucrose

diamond
by white diamond.
Juice droplets
crystalize
upon my lips,
candy hexagons.
Or like the chemistry

of kissing & kissing King Midas:
the cold process
of becoming precious
metal. Each cell
calcifies; petrifies
into the color
of bliss, of sunset

until even your bangs
feel like the band
of a ruby encrusted
crown: crash
after the high.

Two Erotic Sonnets
Sheri Lohr

A Walled Garden

In the hidden inner court, a tree
is artfully espaliered on the wall:
slim branch and scarlet bloom the gardener's thrall.
As you lie in sun there, think of me.
You are my dragonfly in amber. Be
a butterfly on black velvet, impaled;
a ship that's held at anchor, with furled sail.
Be kept; be held; submit to ecstasy.

Think of me. See the tree's perfected form
made more lovely by the discipline
pinning graceful limbs against the bricks.
Think of me and close your eyes and warm
yourself. Recall the carpet with your skin
where my hands gripped and pinned your willing wrists.

The Stair

The newel post is hard and smooth to hand
and then the banister, with python grace
is undulating to her palm's caress,
as all the rails at rapt attention stand.
The wood warms at a fingertip's demand.
Her arching, slippered foot upon the tread
climbs step by step toward the waiting bed
in the chamber where the tryst is planned.

Her brushing thighs, covertly draped in cotton lace,
ignite in secret with each riser gained,
so each one blushes sweetly to her mate.
The highest step is promising embrace,
and turning down the linen counterpane
she slips between the scented sheets to wait.

Stars

Ray Campbell

The night was crawling all over us
With silvery tendrils of whispered love.
The air breathed magic.
Dawn was an orange surprise,
Too soon, unexpected.
You left stars in my bed
Smelling like eternity and you.

I slept in the luxurious emptiness.
I awoke to a silly grin in my mirror.
I found my Cheerios tasted better.
The milk was colder, fresher.
The day was not alive,
It was ... bursting.
I was in love with ...
Everything.
All because
You left stars in my bed.

Sleeping with the Poet
C.S. Gilbert

I.
You teach me
it is art to learn
to hear silence.

I love light brightening through lace,
the relentless rheostat of dawn in dapples
as I half-wake and turn in your bed.

Help me to hear silence
smell swamp birds
see the scent of lime, and clear air,
smell sheets slick and soft with wear,
feel cinnamon heat, and the seam of where
nothing
becomes something on a day of solitude.

Teach me to throw back the light, snug quilt
of last night
and bear my bare self to the chill embrace
of this morning's air.

II.
Time hoods eyes and hobbles steps
but instinct stands prime, still true,
awakening at 2 a.m.
in the warm tangle of quilt and limbs,
a leg leaning into mine, the luscious weight
of a melon breast against my shoulder.
I extricate myself as gently as I pulled the nipple
from the sleeping jaws of my newborns,

slowly, barely breathing, beatified.
She sighs the small half-cry I hear
only when she sleeps.
Soundless on the carpet,
careful she does not wake,
I do not kiss her goodbye.
On the street stars blaze
subversive against city lights,
and contentment sings me home.

III.
Late the night I knew I could no longer love the poet,
or rather, I could love the poet but not be with her,
or rather (it is a very small town) I could be with her
but not make love to her,
I drove home, ate grapefruit, and decided
not to write a poem.

My Only Love. Poem.
Erin Francis

He turned
and was above me—
like the sun and stars—
and all else above me—
and he did it silently—
and made me studder—
and took my breath—
Took my breath under blankets,
and darkness
and kissed me—
with such strength and sureness—
I would have lost balance if standing.

Iris di Fireze
Theresa Carr

From your rhizomes in the soil
To the air you cleanse,
You lend magnificence to the landscape.
The triumvirates of your sepals
Standards
Stamens and
Styles
Gives to symmetry grace.
The dark dark purple black
Color of your petals
Startles the mind with its clarity,
And brings the blood to my lips.
Your falls droop,
A banner calling my name
A promise
A covenant
A thing to come.
The stature of your corolla
Is a crown like no other.
Etched in my heart mind
Are the tender lengths of your crests,
The display on your sepals of light purple tresses.
I tremble to touch your stem,
While your stalk reverberates in kind.
My fingertips burn yet
From the press of your fronds.
I need no longer yearn for that
Which is given to me.
Holding your calyx
I travel down your white throat
To kiss the golden yellow pollen
That has ached for my touch.

God
Alex Symington

as i fade away

i catch a glimpse

a flash of hips

red lips

exaltation in our

cellular manifestation

oh yes there is

a god

she is the power and

the glory

chestnut hair swinging

sunlit and gleaming

she with her man

there is hope in

those hips

a mortal gamble

for immortality

belly taut and round

animal instinct

the future of man

is woman

The Importance of Feathers
Flower Conroy

The plane of a feather seems seamless.
A duck or a dove's feather is

distinct as a thumbprint or iris,
from that of a ptarmigan.

Most extraordinary breed:
natures male magnificent-bird-of

paradise, sporting metallic-green bib,
a golden cape & bare curl-

ing quills. What costumes! Extravagantly
long pennants, the flared crests, names

borrowed from royalty: Prince Rudolph's
blue; King of Saxony; Little

king. To think some choking sire,
his little egghead peeking from nest

of ruffles, he mimicking the bird's garb
then naming the bird after

himself! Alas, lovely; I've been
mischievous, distracting you so

when we both know the only feather
of importance is this quill I

dip & scribe down the length
of your shivering dreamy molted body

hot blue skin calligraphy

Running with the Bull
Marci Rose

My Brahma Bull
You Graze Patiently and enjoy
The Sun
Your thick mane is warm and strong
A red flag flits by, An Orange Skirt
A glance of mistrust
An ounce of fear
An air of uncertainty
You Snort, You Stomp
You Smoke, You Steam
You Stampede
I dance around you
Putting out the flames
Patting out my fear, doubt, and uncertainty
Side Stepping your anger
Trying to blanketedly trust
Longing to feel Peace in our
Dance Together
Quiet, warmth, knowing trust
My Fingers through your mane
Waiting to find reassurance in
Your gaze
Not truth in your anger
The red flag is waived
The Dance Begins again
The Bulls nature is angry
The Matador's nature is mistrust
They Tango, they Salsa, they Hustle
They need each other
They show each other
Reassurance, Trust Loyalty
LOVE and Dance the Time-Honored Dance

Rippin'
Ray Campbell

A perfect pair of rips.
One in her jeans,
          showing skin and dreams.
And one in my heart,
          Showing hope and more.

I want to slide my finger
Along the edge of what nature shows,
To tickle and arouse.
I want to take her somewhere...
Private.
I want her to know multiple rips.
I want to hear her rip my name
On the top of her lungs.
I want to rip her night into shreds.

I want to wake to find
Ripped sheets, blankets, pillows, and her,
With her breath
Ripplin' the hair on my chest.
 I want to see the sun come up in her eyes,
See her eyes smile that sunrise
When she whispers,
"Rippin'!"

Remembering
Nance Boylan

Flickering eyes
    chattering lips
  anticipated breath

swell of wet belly,
  knot in thigh
dancing tongue dies

  In the dark, blushed and ashamed
I no longer think of you

Sunday Sundae
Pam Strother

Lust is like ice cream, he said.
Sitting in beach chairs on the dock,
I thought it was his poet's soul that spoke,
not his bad marriage.
There is no unsatisfactory ice cream, he said,
only gradations from mediocre to sublime.

How original, I thought,
listening to his wife's voice weaving
through the conversation up on the porch.
She, the less accessible of the two,
mummified in thirty years' connubial bliss,
already knew his sins.

Seductively separate
from his Neapolitan fantasies,
his pistachio dreams with whipped cream
and cherries,
the lake water ripples
smoothing desire.

Now invisible and naked and slaked I crawl
Flower Conroy

from the dipping pool's belly onto the underwater ledge:
tropical afternoon weekday sunlight tattered by the palm
frond's fringe makes shadow skeletons, flexible bones

of light's blockage on the patio pavers. Among the leaves
Jackson Pollock splatters of sun so that shadow moves
into light, light slips into shadow, what is bright is exchanged

for what is dull, what is dull is broken into what is bright.
My white parts glow, the migrating birds spy before taking
flight, the mechanical waterfall taunts gravity, the dog sips

from my plastic stem of ice water, sneezes, again laps.
Overhead, sky is a mindless, lighthearted blue without
cloud though the occasional plane slits across it. I pick

up my book. It's the same story. A daydreamer dreaming
about the dreams of the rich & famous, daydreaming about
being rich & famous, what being rich & famous tastes like-

does it taste like this? Does it taste like late spring on an island,
when the buds begin to spill their odor, does it taste like the beetle
between the grackle's beak, the condensation of this cup of cool

water sweating in the sweet & wooly late afternoon sun, does it
taste like the waxy sunshine pooling in the cupping hands of leaves,
does it taste like the freedom of being naked & invisible in my

backyard, wasting a few hours with a book while the sun scatters
splinters of light on my glowing shoulders, does it taste like the water
in my hair, on my lips, like you, covered in sweat & tired, coming

home early to find me, does it taste like that this ecstasy, like raw
day broken open & sucked, like my body greeting your body, how
lips & skin taste bitter, like yolk, like a dream spoiling in the acid sun?

Opiate
Alex Symington

As I read you, so you read me

We are wet words, glistening

Tear drop in mid air, gentle warm

Circling finger and tongue

Lips apart, softly singing

Me to you, you to me

Eyes closed and open, taking turns

A moment of clarity

More powerful than gravity

A nameless opiate of our formless world

Chapter 5

Bird of Paradise

Joyful

Separation Blues
(for Roz, with a nod toward Auden's "Funeral Blues")
Allen Meece

Stop all the clocks and pullout the phones!
Put the calendar ahead to August and don't look at it anymore.
Don't sell gas, let traffic die.
Open the doors, leave trash in the street, neither recycle nor buy.

Cannonball the neighbor's TV, cut the cord, let 'em sweat.
There is no motion here but that of the spheres.
Take the cold stuff out of the fridge, unplug it too.
Abandon Coral City and don't forget;

The fair Ms. Brackenbury has gone away.

Guide a hurricane down Antilles' corridor!
Let it pound the shore, submerge the trees.
Debris the structures, float 'em out to sea.
Vines and rust shall cover The Rock 'til she comes home to me.

I'll build her a dock, her dainty foot to tread,
alighting from her boat.
A narrow path in the tangled forest leading to my door.
Now, start one generator and turn one fan, spinning over the bed.
She's traveled far and earned a rest, a place to lay her head.

Start the clocks and plug-in the phones—tomorrow

It could have been the number 3
Matt Lynch

It could have been the number 3

with its yuca and tamale tucked in alongside steaming garlic roast pork

or maybe the perfect margarita or 2

quenching the thirst of a sultry summer afternoon

or was it any morning on the White Street pier

an artist's pallet bursting forth with each passing second

as the sun rises on yet another tropical day

snorkeling with snook by the rocks just off the beach

ice cold beer hidden in a cooler on the beach

SSSSSSHHHHHHHHHHHHHH

do not tell anyone

the reason why

I love Key West

the reason I stopped counting weekends

after the first one 16 years ago

that was just a visit

that turned to eternity

and made me believe

in love

once more

Down There
Rachel Scott

There's a place I love that's way down south
'bout as far as the road can go.
 I go there when I need some time
To kick it back and take it slow.
I don't love it for the Duval Crawl
Or sunset in the square.
I love it for the peace of mind I find when I'm down there.

The quiet shade down Elizabeth Street,
The slap of flip-flops on my feet,
The smell of salty ocean air,
Gentle trade winds in my hair,
All make me want to stay another day.

This place I love, it's far, far south,
In fact, it's the end of the road.
It's where I go to finally get
The relaxation that I'm owed.
I don't go there for the snorkel tour,
Or to ride the damn Conch Train.
I go there to facilitate
Down time for my brain.

The Goombay as she rides the tides,
Water slapping at her sides.
The creaking of the mooring line,
In the cockpit drinking wine.
All make me want to stay another week.

Oh, there's a place I love that's way down south,
As far as the road will go.

I go there and make some time
For kicking back and going slow.
I don't love it for the real estate,
I ain't buyin' no condo.

Only locals know.
The serenity of summertime,
Cold Corona, extra lime.
Chickens up and down the block,
Big 'ol tarpon at the dock
All make me want to come and stay
Forever…
Yeah, maybe I could go and stay Forever.

Barbados
Dan Mehler

The moonlight highlights our lives tonight
In palm tree shadows we hide
Interwoven souls lying in the sand
The stars dance naked wooing a passive sky
The water glistens then sparks as we touch
While time races by laughing, unconcerned
With the two of us

Some Lover or Other
Sheri Lohr

I loved you madly,
I loved you wild.
I loved you like a demon,
I loved you like a child.
I loved you as we biked along
the road beside the beach.
I loved you when the full moon seemed
almost within our reach.

I loved you rocking on the waves
that splashed against the hull.
I loved you when we lay in sand
and watched a diving gull.
I loved you at the Green Parrot Bar,
dancing drunk and dazed.
I loved you at 4AM under the stars,
and bringing you home amazed.

I loved you laughing in the streets,
and watching the parade.
I loved you tangled in the sheets,
where you were sweetly laid.
I loved you wearing all your faces.
I whispered all your names.
I loved you and lost you a hundred times
but I loved you truly, all the same.

Mock Chicken Legs
Jack Hackett

Mock Chicken legs
in gravy; potatoes, yeah
whipped the way you sometimes do
peas little peas
yes orange jello with
shaved carrots
butter cream cake
strawberry filled
ooohh the day
that ritual day
waking in the morning
with a present maybe two
at your feet knowing
you get to pick what to eat tonight
 oh the day that ritual day
sittin at the head of the table
served first
lights out candles all aglow
make a wish   blow
happy birthday
oh i love birthdays.

I've Got Nothing On But the Radio
T.J. Allen (Trinidad Joe)

You got dressed this morning
About a half past dawn.
When I asked, "How long you're going?"
You said you won't be gone long.
I don't know where you went
Or why you had to go,
So I'll still be lying here
With nothing on but the radio.

The milkman came and went
I heard the mailman come and go,
When are you coming back
I still don't know.
So I'll still be lying here
With nothing on but the radio.

I heard a car drive up
So I ran and opened the door,
I didn't see you
But guess what the neighbors saw!

Now it's way past noon
It's late afternoon,
Baby, please come back
Come home soon!

The sun went down
And the moon started to shine,
Baby, please hurry home
And again be mine!

Damn, it's dawn again
And you still didn't show,
And I'll still be lying here
With nothing on but the radio!

Strings
Peggy Butler

For many years I had thought my life was not my own;
    somewhere,
someone else was turning the key to every door I opened;
I had no control over the direction I was taking
No matter that I wanted something good, someone with strength
to hold onto, to love; that thing, that thing was always there,
    reaching out
from the dark, from below (from above?), taking from me,
snatching, turning, changing.

Many times I've cried, I've screamed, I've begged: Please, please,
    just this once,
let it be my move; just this once let this ship be steered by my
    hands, my mind,
my desires, my dreams. But, no.
Whatever possessed me to think that I could be that master, that
    director,
even that actor?
No, I was just the puppet, and that thing—it pulled the strings.

But wait! Somehow, somewhere along the way, I must have ...
Here I was, wanting you, thinking of you, dreaming
that the warm feeling (love?) I had in your presence would be,
could be reciprocated, but afraid that it is up there (down there?)
planning, scheming, negotiating the turns away from you,
because I have no right (do I?) to make my own move toward
    you.

Then, today I knew, I really knew that, somehow, somewhere
    along the way,
I must have cut the strings, because today, right now,
you're sitting there,
watching, smiling, loving me.

Come on See
Tony W. Collins

Together we travel
Thoughts we unravel
Defeat the beast
Share the feast
Table we prepare
Love we share
Cups we fill
Truly God's will
Firm we stand
Reach your hand
Have no fear
We are here
Gathering the lost
There's no cost
It's always free
Come on see
We are one.
God's only Son
Jesus will talk
We only walk
Learn and listen
His eyes glisten
You can be
Part of We
Come on see
It's always free

The Alphabet of Sea Terns
Cricket Desmarais

Aves in aria, one morning the beach filled up
with skimmers, row upon row of Rynchops niger,
birds loafing the coast in their little black hats,

red mandibles gleaming amid graceful flight.
The steady beat of long wings with my prayers
sung out over them-when they flew away, they

took the past with them. That night we learned
the tipped curve and belly of "a," both the eager first
letter and a sigh that makes music where music

once wasn't, satisfaction found and released
into air, dewy with longing despite itself. With
"a" came anemone, atoms, affinity. To our

surprise, later amnion, areola, abdomen–
astonishing- that they grow darker and larger
each day. But will I still love the night sky when

you arrive, still care about tide-pools and sea-terns?
My mother never spoke of such things, though she read
stars like a book never shelved. We lived our days by

them, packed under their dim glimmer when a man
shook her up or left a dark mark. Then the sea took over,
told me to call it home. I spent years trying to find

the right shoreline, uncertain yet calmed by the steady change
of tides. This, I thought, I could trust. Trust no one,
cried the gulls. Now the lights are in my eye, made

bright by salt and the confidence of heliotropes,
doing what they do by instinct alone. Still, I am
human. I think too much. In five months, it will all

make sense, your creamy newness will slide out of hiding
to breathe on your own. You, my eager first, found
and released into air, coming from two who love
the sea, from satisfaction, from the sigh-
making music dewy with longing and the perfect
convergence when you choose to let go.

My Love She's Like
Jack Hackett

she's like
the sweet, sweet, wind
that blows on you
during the hot summertime
she's like
the blossom on the tree
after the cold, cold winters gone
she's like
the river cross your feet
after hiking all the day long
she's like
a warm campfire light
in the middle of chilled nite
she's' like everything
everything that seems good to me
but then she turns
turns and turns
then she's like
a nail coming through
your only pair of shoes
like a little baby
spitting up all over you
she's like cold burnt toast
you know she's like the worst
then she turns, turns and turns
and she's that
sweet, sweet wind
that blows on you
during the hot summer time
she's that blossom on the tree
after the cold winters gone

she's that river cross your feet
after hiking all the day long
she's that warm campfire light
in the middle of a chilled night
she's everything, everything
everything that seems good to me

Bright Silken Tents
Allen Meece

This touchingness,
this reciprocity of sharing
this openess, piercing
all that we are.

These miraculous bodies
offered totally.
Seeds and eggs,
microcosms of life,
freely united.

And these minds,
infinite computers,
perceiving all concepts,
dedicated to the joy of loving

And finally, the souls,
bright silken tents
erected against the darkness.
We ask another inside
and light a candle
to share the paradise.

It's an amazing life,
played out among the stars of deepest space.
But the most wondrous thing
--I can't get over it --
is just this touchingness.

7 Caveats in May
(after Maxine Kumin and Edith Piaf)
C.S. Gilbert

One: pay proper homage to the Maypole;
        dance with joy, and flirt

Two: do not be cool to him or her
        whose eyes caught yours in flight
        and did a double-take

Three: do not shrink from the electric shock
        of his/her skin brushing yours
        on the next pass

Four: when the pole is woven into rainbows,
        do not deny the mead and the May wine,
        do not fail to nibble cakes from each other's fingers
        and lick off the frosting

Five: do not linger to feast's end, weave fingers and leave;
        find the tall, new grass,
        not yet scythed

Six: do not fail, in your soft bower, to love lustily
        until Morpheus lures you to sleep softly
        in each other's arms.

Seven: Regret nothing.

TJ Allen (aka Trinidad Joe) *Nothing on But the Radio;* Before going on his tour of many European countries, he performed from Alaska to Argentina. TJ did a special performance in Egypt between the pyramids and the Sphinx. He took the time to write his initials in the sands of the Sahara Desert.

Steve Allerton *How I Loved You; Island of You;* Steve Allerton is from New York and a graduate of The Taylor School of Art in Philadelphia. He has lived in Key West since the early eighties as an artist and musician writing the poetry of song lyrics.

Vicki Boguszewski *Key West in Another Neighborhood;* Vicki Boguszewski, a member of the Key West Poetry Guild since 1996, published a collection of original poetry and art entitled "Mesource" in 2008; she is at home in Key West, FL.

Nance Boylan *Late Night Poem; Unraveling; In the Pink Morning Hour; Unraveling; Remembering;* Nance Boylan–Inspired by the art, creative energy, and all the magnificent colors, moved to Key West in 2010 to write poetry in earnest.

Rosiland Brackenbury *Valentine's Day, Years On; Solstice; At Key West Bight;* Rosalind was born in England and has lived in Key West since 1993 with her husband Allen Meece. Her latest poetry book "The Joy of the Nearly Old" is available from Hanging Loose Press, Brooklyn, NY.

Eric Brockmyer *My Second Spring; Through the White Linen;* Eric Brockmyer, a mid-west transplant, started writing poetry on his wooden pirate ship in Key West after retiring from the military.

Mark Burgin *Sharon*

Peggy Butler *Strings;* Peggy Butler, former Key West resident, now in mainland South Florida, is a three-time winner in the KWWG Short Story Contest, retired RN, mother, grandmother and great-grandmother, who covered the Key West City Commission as a free-lance reporter, and is the author of *Starfish;* her memoir, *And*

Then There Was One, will be released in the summer of 2012.

Omar Calleja *If Only You Knew;* Omar is a third generation Conch who has been writing poems since the late sixties which he calls "Pogo Stick," poetry reflecting the ups and downs of humanity.

Ray Campbell *Only a Woman; Rippin' ; Stars; WD40 for my Soul;* Ray Campbell has been writing poetry his whole life, sometimes even successfully.

Theresa Carr *On the Brink of White Coral; Iris di Firenze;* Theresa Carr is a Lebenskunstlerin who suffers from Wanderlust; in English that means she is a snow bard, the type that creeps out of the mangroves.

Tony W. Collins *Come On See* ; Poetry has always been a best friend to Tony Collins. His work is influenced by nature and John Lennon.

Kirby Congdon *At the Edge; For a Friend; For Ralph Simmons Jr.; On a Death;* Kirby Congdon has no rationale for his commitment to poetry, but he says he will look for one.

Flower Conroy *Now Invisible and Naked and Slaked I Crawl; Precious Luscious; The Importance of Feathers; Unquenching;* Flower Conroy writes poetry.

Cricket Desmarais *Goodbye Passion (Flower); Pink; The Alphabet of Sea Terns;* Cricket Desmarais is a writer, consultant, coach and yoga instructor living with her family in Key West, Fl. She is dedicated to living—and helping others live—a more luminous and joyful life, as simply and sanely as possible.

Katherine Doughty *Bougainvilla; Catch and Release; doing time;* Katharine Doughty, raised in New Jersey, attended the first Dodge Poetry Festival there in 1986. A resident of Key West since 2003, she writes, creates visual art and practices massage therapy.

Lisa Ermine *If I Could Trade;* Lisa Ermine is married and lives in Big Pine Key, Fl. Author since 1980. Retired "Easter Morning."

Carol Fran *Before The Day*

Erin Francis *My Only Love. Poem.*

C.S. Gilbert *7 Caveats in May; Saying Au Revoir; Sleeping with the Poet; Thomas Street;* C.S. Gilbert is a recovering college teacher, semi-retired activist, journalist and arts critic currently at work on her second and third books of poetry.

Sarah Goodwin-Nguyen *Icarus;* Sarah Goodwin-Nguyen works as an eco-tour guide by bike and by kayak. Her poetry has appeared in *Secret of Salt, Best of Wicked Alice, Long shot, Fuel, Stray Dog* and more.

Jack Hackett *Mock Chicken Legs; My Love She's Like;* Tortuga Jack Hackett, is a poet sailor, a story teller and a musician. En route to St Croix in the eighties, he visited Key West and has been a resident ever since. He has won the Ernest Hemingway Story Teller's competition more than once.

Susan S. Keiser *Oliva Street Prayers; Redox Pair; Tin-Roof Cradle* Susan S. Keiserís work has appeared in a number of journals including *Haggard and Halloo, SpokenWar, The Camel Saloon, Orion Headless,* and *amphibi.us.* She is currently at work on an original screenplay.

Deborah Linker *Orchids at Midnight; Strong as Lily;* Deborah Linker, co-author of a series of "Poetry Readings of The Keys" and producer of the "Open Mic Poetry Jam" of the Marathon public library and is currently working on a collection of poems, "Living on the Edge."

Sheri Lohr *Key West, I Love You; Astral Light; Some Lover or Other; Two Erotic Sonnets;* Sheri Lohr, former sailor, scuba instructor and steam plant operator, owns a small publishing company in Key West, assisted by Pascal, a very intelligent poodle.

Matt Lynch *It Could Have been the Number 3;* Matt Lynch ran aground in Key West sometime towards the end of the last century.

Allen Meece *Bright Silken Tents; Give Me No Tomorrows; Separation Blues;* Allen has been involved with the Key West Poetry Guild since its meetings were held in the Guild Hall Art Gallery in 1977. His poems often contain bold confrontational tones.

Dan Mehler *Barbados;* I'm a middle aged helpless romantic unpublished poet. I live in Coral Springs, FL and own a plant nursery called Johnny Mangoes in Delray Beach, FL. I spend three months in the summer in Key West.

Lucy Miranda *Hope Deferred;* Inspired by love as it never fails.

Tod Perry *A Friend Speaks of Unrequited Love;* Tod Perry, a graduate of the Iowa Writers Workshop, lives part of the year on Cudjoe Key, and his poems and translations have appeared in various publications.

Marci L. Rose *Running with the Bull;* Marci L. Rose is a Dirt Lawyer, Hatha Yoga Teacher, Avid Tree Hugger, and soon to be a Doctor of Naturopathic Medicine.

Rachel Scott *Down There*

Sarah Shea *Valentine's Day at Sea;* Sara Shea is a poet and writer with a business background. Sara's poem in this anthology was written here in Key West while she was artist in residence at Mockingbird Studio.

Pamela A. Strother *Long Love; On opening mail from Joannie on Friday; Sunday Sundae;* Pamela A. Strother, Ph.D, retired university teacher and practicing psychotherapist of thirty years has been writing poems since the first grade. Her first chapbook, *Here at the End of the Road, Key West Poems* (SeaStory Press) was published in 2007

Alex Symington *God; Hummingbird; Methods; Opiate;* Alex Symington is a poet/anthropologist wannabe and is attempting to remain teachable in his old age. He loves in Key West with his wife, Anna.

Leonel F. Valle *Blue Sandals; Duval Street Gal; Key West; Winter;* Leonel F. Valle is an award-winning poet who writes about the Florida Keys.

J.M. Varela *Phoenix; Reality and Dreams; When Love Dies;* J.M. Varela, Conch poet, (aka Jean Gregory) island born and bred tells true, historic Key West stories you won't hear on the Conch Train.

Malcom Willison *Equinox Brief Encounter; Remainders;* Malcom Willison has spent a lifetime writing poetry and publishing some of it. He spends his time between Key West, New Orleans and up-state New York.